BEYONDRHYTHMGUITAR
LICKSRIFFS&FILLS

Build Riffs, Fills & Solos Around the Most Important Chord Shapes in Rock & Blues Guitar

SIMONPRATT

FUNDAMENTALCHANGES

Beyond Rhythm Guitar: Licks, Riffs and Fills

Build Riffs, Fills & Solos Around the Most Important Chord Shapes in Rock & Blues Guitar

Published by **www.fundamental-changes.com**

ISBN: 978-1-911267-92-8

Copyright © 2017 Simon Pratt

www.fundamental-changes.com

Twitter: **@guitar_joseph**

Over 10,000 fans on Facebook: **FundamentalChangesInGuitar**

Instagram: **FundamentalChanges**

For over 350 Free Guitar Lessons with Videos Check Out

www.fundamental-changes.com

Cover Image Copyright: Shutterstock: Roman Voloshyn

Contents

Introduction   4

Get the Audio   5

Section One: Essentials   6

Chapter One – Open Major Chords   6
Core Concepts for Blending Rhythm and Lead Guitar   7
C Major Fills   10
D Major Fills   12
A Major Fills   14
E Major Fills   16

Chapter Two – Open Minor Chords   18
A Minor Fills   20
D Minor Fills   22

Chapter Three – Capo Chords   30
Buying a Capo   30
C-Shape fills   31
A-Shape fills   32
G-Shape fills   34
E-Shape fills   36
D-Shape fills   37
A Minor-Shape fills   39
Open E Minor-Shape fills   40
Open D Minor-Shape fills   41
Essential capo listening   43

Section Two: Blues   44

Chapter Four – Blues Part One   44
'Riffy' Twelve-Bar Blues   52

Chapter Five – Minor Blues   60

Chapter Six – Gospel Blues   72
A Mixolydian Lick Vocabulary   75
D Mixolydian Scale Licks   79
E Mixolydian Scale Licks   80

Section 3: Rock   83

Chapter Seven – Two-Note Power Chords   83

Chapter Eight – Power Chords Part Two   92
B Minor Lick Vocabulary   94
B Major Lick Vocabulary   99

Chapter Nine – Drone Notes   110
Checklist   121

Conclusion   122
Pop Quiz Answers   122

Introduction

Imagine walking into your local guitar shop and picking up your favourite guitar. Sitting down to play it you hear Stairway to Heaven to your right, Sweet Child O' Mine to your left and Wonderwall in front of you. As soon as you go to play, all the countless hours of learning songs and pieces seem to go out the window. In my teaching I refer to this as "guitar shop syndrome". Of course, this is not only limited to the guitar shop but anywhere an element of performance is needed.

Although learning songs and pieces is an essential part of learning the guitar, becoming a master of combining chords and lead guitar fills is the only sure way to never suffer 'guitar shop syndrome' again!

In this book you will learn how to blend open chords, capo chords, power chords, double-stops, triads, and barre chords with corresponding scale shapes and licks.

I have split this book into genre-based sections for ease of reference. Section One is Essentials and concentrates on the open and capo chords that are associated with acoustic and folk playing. Section Two focuses on Blues, and Section Three on Rock.

If you are new to blending rhythm and lead guitar, I recommend you work through the book from start to finish, that way you will learn and develop your skills in a logical way. If you are already adept at these techniques and are just looking for fresh ideas, then feel free to dive into any chapter you wish!

This book is packed full of ideas to inspire you to be as creative as possible. I recommend learning my examples and highlighting your particular favorites, before using those as a template to create your own ideas.

In your practice regime combine playing on your own, with a metronome, with drum tracks, with backing tracks, and with other musicians. This makes for a well-rounded practice time that will help you apply the techniques and ideas featured this book.

The audio for this book is available from www.fundamental-changes.com. Get it so you can hear how I play and *phrase* each example.

Happy Playing!

Simon

* All examples featured in this book are in 4/4 time unless otherwise stated *

Get the Audio

The audio files for this book are available to download for free from **www.fundamental-changes.com** and the link is in the top right corner of the site. Simply select this book title from the drop-down menu and follow the instructions to get the audio.

We recommend that you download the files directly to your computer, not to your tablet, and extract them there before adding them to your media library. You can then put them on your tablet, iPod or burn them to CD. There is a help PDF on the download page, and we provide technical support via the contact form.

Twitter: @guitar_joseph

Over 10,000 fans on Facebook: FundamentalChangesInGuitar

Instagram: FundamentalChanges

For over 350 Free Guitar Lessons with Videos Check Out

www.fundamental-changes.com

Section One: Essentials
Chapter One – Open Major Chords

An open chord is simply one that contains one or more open strings. They have a distinctive ringing quality to them and have been used across multiple genres including pop, folk, rock, and country. In this chapter I will show you how to pair open chords with corresponding scale shapes, and blend rhythmic patterns with licks and fills. The chords included in this chapter are the fundamental open major chord shapes of G, C, D, A, and E.

Although studying open chords may seem basic, the concepts in this chapter are the building blocks for all future chapters. By studying how each example is created, you will be able to apply the ideas into your own playing and composition, which is of course the aim of this entire book!

I recommend you listen to each audio example before playing through the ideas featured in this chapter. Take your time to learn and digest all the material: there is no rush!

If you are unfamiliar with open chord shapes, or would like a reminder, I recommend Joseph Alexander's book *The First 100 Chords for Guitar.*

Example 1a demonstrates an open G Major chord and a G Major Pentatonic (G A B D E) scale using open strings. The open G Major Pentatonic seen here will be used in a lot of examples, so be sure to internalise it before moving on.

Example 1a

Core Concepts for Blending Rhythm and Lead Guitar

Strum an open G Major chord twice and add the "mini fill" formed from the open G Major Pentatonic scale. The pattern used here is 'strum, strum, fill.' This is a useful pattern to remember, and as you progress, you will be able to use it on any chord and corresponding scale shape.

Example 1b

Once again, strum the open G Major chord twice but add the fill on the D and G strings using the open G Major Pentatonic scale.

Example 1c

You can combine the previous two examples to create a two bar 'strum and lick' pattern. This is popular in folk and country music.

In example 1d, start with a fill in the open G Major Pentatonic and then strum the G Major chord twice.

Example 1d

Now play fill two before strumming the open G Major chord twice.

Example 1e

By combining the previous two examples, we can create a two-bar pattern using the "fill before strum" method.

Instead of strumming the whole G Major chord, example 1f introduces a small arpeggio pattern followed by a fill using the open G Major chord and G Major Pentatonic.

Example 1f

Example 1g blends an open G Major Pentatonic fill on the D and G strings with the previous arpeggiated G Major chord.

Example 1g

To create a two-bar phrase you can combine the previous two examples. This pattern is arpeggio – fill 1 – arpeggio – fill 2.

Play the open G Major Pentatonic fill before the G Major arpeggio to reverse the previous patterns.

Example 1h

Now use fill two before playing the open G Major chord arpeggio pattern.

Example 1i

You can combine the previous two examples to form a two-bar G Major rhythm and lead pattern.

C Major Fills

Example 1j shows an open C Major chord, followed by an open C Major Pentatonic scale (C D E G A).

Example 1j

It is important to learn to move the patterns you know into different keys. In example 1k, strum the open C Major chord twice before playing the mini fill using the open C Major Pentatonic scale.

Example 1k

Next, strum the C Major chord twice before playing the fill on the G and B strings using the C Major Pentatonic scale.

Example 1l

To make a two-bar pattern, combine the previous two examples. You can also reverse the two bars to create another common pop pattern. By starting with a fill before strumming you can change the feel of the rhythmic pattern completely.

Example 1m

Play an open C Major chord arpeggio before playing alternating fills in example 1n.

Example 1n

Now play the fills before the open C Major arpeggio once again using the open C Major Pentatonic scale.

Example 1o

D Major Fills

Play an open D Major chord, followed by an open D Major Pentatonic scale (D E F# A B).

Example 1p

Strum an open D Major chord twice before playing fills using the open D Major Pentatonic scale.

Example 1q

Play the fills before strumming the chords in example 1s.

Example 1r

By picking the notes of the D Major chord individually we create a mini arpeggio, which is followed by D Major Pentatonic scale fills.

Example 1s

Now that you have mastered these individual chord shapes, and their corresponding scales and fills, it is time to look at a full chord sequence using the chords of G, C, and D. The same pattern happens in every bar: a syncopated strumming pattern for two beats and then two beats of fill. This open chord pattern of G, C, and D is one of the most common in rock and pop, so learn my example but also write your own ideas too.

Example 1t

A Major Fills

Play the Open A Major chord followed by the open A Major pentatonic scale (A B C# E F#).

Example 1u

Strum the open A Major chord twice before playing the fills using the open A Major Pentatonic scale.

Example 1v

Play the fills using the open A Major Pentatonic scale before strumming on open A Major chord twice.

Example 1w

In this example, arpeggiate the open A Major chord before adding the fill at the end of each bar.

Example 1x

E Major Fills

This example shows an open E Major chord and the open E Major Pentatonic scale shape (E F# G# B C#).

Example 1y

Now strum an open E Major chord twice before applying fills using the open E Major Pentatonic scale.

Example 1z

This time reverse the previous example by starting each bar with a fill before strumming the E Major chord twice.

Example 1za

The final example demonstrates playing an E Major arpeggio before using a fill from the open E Major Pentatonic scale.

Example 1zb

This chapter, I have shown some fundamental ways to blend open string-chords with open-string scale licks. These patterns will work for any chord, not just open chords, as long as you know the correct scale to play.

Shown below is a chart of the fill patterns used in this chapter. This will be a reference point for you when building your own ideas.

Pattern	Number of Bars
Strum Strum Fill 1	1
Strum Strum Fill 2	1
Strum Strum Fill 1 | Strum Strum Fill 2	2
Fill 1 Strum Strum	1
Fill 2 Strum Strum	1
Fill 1 Strum Strum | Fill 2 Strum Strum	2

Chapter Two – Open Minor Chords

In this chapter, we will learn how to add fills to minor chords.

Example 2a demonstrates an open E Minor chord followed by an open E Blues scale (E G A Bb B D). If you would prefer to play a standard E Minor Pentatonic scale (E G A B D) leave out the notes with brackets around them.

Example 2a

In this example, I demonstrate a syncopated strumming pattern on an E Minor chord, followed by a rest and a fill using the open E Blues scale. Including a rest between rhythm and lead ideas helps you stay in time, especially at higher speeds. As with all the examples in this book, listen to the audio tracks before playing them to see how I phrase each one.

Example 2b

I always ensure I can play any lick many ways before I move on to learn new material. In example 2c we play the E Blues scale fills before the syncopated strums, and add a rest and the end of each bar.

Example 2c

A concept I want to highlight early on is the idea of playing 'double-stops' (two notes played at the same time). Normally when we play a fill we use single notes, but by including double-stop ideas our lick vocabulary becomes wider. Example 2d revolves around the open E Blues scale and an open E Minor chord.

Example 2d

Reverse the previous example to create another open E Minor double-stop phrase.

Example 2e

A Minor Fills

Play an open A Minor chord followed by the open A Blues scale (A C D Eb E G).

Example 2f

Now play this syncopated A Minor chord sequence followed by two fills that use the open A Blues scale.

Example 2g

Start with some open A Blues scale fills before playing a syncopated strumming pattern on the A Minor chord.

Example 2h

Example 2i is a busy idea that combines double-stops and a fill using the A Blues scale.

Example 2i

Pick the root of the A Minor chord before strumming the higher four strings, then play the double-stop fills using the open A Blues scale.

Example 2j

D Minor Fills

In example 2k play the open D Minor chord before playing and memorising the D Blues scale.

Example 2k

Now apply a different syncopated strumming pattern on the D Minor chord before playing fills with the open D Blues scale.

Example 2l

Play the D Blues fills before the syncopated open D Minor chords.

Example 2m

Here in example 2n, I have created a D Minor vamp that uses the open D string and double-stop patterns within the Blues scale.

Example 2n

Vary the tone you use to play the examples in this book. Try using distortion, a clean sound, or play on an acoustic guitar.

Example 2o

Now that you have learnt individual A minor, D minor and E minor ideas it's time to combine them into a two-bar phrase.

Example 2p

Example 2q uses open A, D, and E minor chords and their corresponding Blues scales to create an intricate two bar pop-rock pattern.

Example 2q

With the more sophisticated patterns, learn a beat or two at a time until these feel fluid and natural. Then, and only then, add another beat or two until you can play the whole pattern without any pauses. Start off slowly, at around 50 beats-per-minute, and use a metronome to keep in time.

Example 2r

Example 2s uses the three chords from the previous chapter G, C, D, and an E Minor to create a common pop chord sequence.

Example 2s

Play a fill before playing two strums on each chord of G, E Minor, C, and D.

Example 2t

Now play an arpeggio on each chord before playing a fill at the end of each bar.

Example 2u

Example 2v demonstrates a longer syncopated strumming pattern on the chords of G, E Minor, C, and D, and applies a fill from their corresponding scale shapes.

Example 2v

Play the fills before the syncopated strumming pattern in this example.

Example 2w

The final example uses double-stops that precede two strums on each chord.

Example 2x

As well as learning the individual examples, take note of how each pattern is built. Use the diagram below as reference when building your own riffs.

Pattern	Number of Bars
Syncopated Strum / Fill	2
Fill / Syncopated Strum	2
Double-Stops and Picked Root note / Strum	2
Pick Root / Strum and Double-Stops	2
Pick Root Strum / Double-Stops	2
Double-Stops / Pick Root Strum	2

Pop Quiz

- What are the notes in the E Blues Scale?

- What is a double-stop?

- What tempo should you start playing these examples at?

- What are the notes in the A Blues Scale?

Answers at the end of the book!

Chapter Three – Capo Chords

Open chords are restricted by their inclusion of an open string, but by adding a capo we can move the open chords to *any* key.

You will learn how to move open chords into new keys by placing a capo at the 4th fret of the guitar. Open chords have a quality that can't be replaced with barre chords, and the examples in this chapter show what can be achieved by using a capo in your playing. Capos work particularly well on an acoustic guitar and when backing a vocalist, especially as a duet.

In this chapter, you can experiment by moving the capo to any fret you wish. If you don't have a capo, you can play each example in its original open position.

I first got into using a capo to create instrumental acoustic pieces after watching Martin Tallstrom's masterpiece **Summer Breeze**.

Buying a Capo

Cheap capos are a waste of money. They normally do not fit well and can make notes sound clunky. I recommend Kyser capos, but most mid-range capos should be sufficient. Remember the adage 'buy cheap, buy twice' when buying gear.

Check out this video lesson I created to see a Kyser capo in action.

www.fundamental-changes.com/creative-capo-chords

Example 3a demonstrates the open Major chord shapes of C A G E and D, but played with the capo at the 4th fret. The chord shape is written above the diagram and the actual chord it creates with the capo is written in brackets. For example, a C shape played with the capo at the 4th fret creates an E Major chord. Strum these open chord shapes along with the accompanying audio track.

Example 3a

Now play the open Minor chords of A Minor, E Minor, and D Minor.

Example 3b

C-Shape fills

The following examples demonstrate fills and rhythmic phrases around the open C Major shape. With the capo placed at the 4th fret, you are playing in the key of E Major.

Example 3c

Example 3d

Example 3e

Example 3f

A-Shape fills

The next examples feature arpeggios, strumming, and fills around the open A Major shape. With the capo on the 4th fret, an open A Major chord shape creates a C# Major chord.

Example 3g

Example 3h

Example 3i

Bands like REM use the following type of picked arpeggios to bring interest to their rhythmic patterns. Note the simple fill in bar four that ties the whole pattern together.

Example 3j

G-Shape fills

The next examples are based around the open G Major shape. With the capo on the 4th fret this creates a B Major chord.

Example 3k is reminiscent of the John Mayer classic Queen of California. The double hammer-on in bar one takes some practice so take your time and work on that separately first.

Example 3k

Example 3l

Example 3m

Example 3n

E-Shape fills

The following examples demonstrate fills and rhythmic phrases around the open E Major chord shape. With the capo placed at the 4th fret you are playing in the key of G# Major.

Bach was noted for his use of descending arpeggio patterns that are similar to the idea demonstrated below.

Example 3o

Example 3p

Example 3q

Example 3r

E (G#)

D-Shape fills

The next examples feature arpeggios, strumming, and fills around the open D Major chord shape. With the capo on the 4th fret an open D Major chord becomes an F# Major chord.

Slash is known for making open chord progressions sound interesting. Listen to the track Knocking on Heavens Door by Guns N' Roses for some open chord magic, then add a capo and play it at the 4th fret.

Example 3s

D (F#)

Example 3t

Double-stops sound fantastic in rock, blues, and country and create a thicker sound than single notes. Example 3u sounds great on an acoustic and an electric, and even works well with distortion.

Example 3u

Example 3v

A Minor-Shape fills

The following examples demonstrate arpeggios, strumming, and fills around on open A Minor shape. With the capo placed at the 4th fret, you are playing in the key of C# Minor. Notice how these examples are similar to the C Major shape fills.

Example 3w

Example 3x

Example 3y

Alternating between a held chord and a fill is a very effective way to blend rhythm and lead ideas. Look at songs you are working on, where can you add fills in between your strums?

Example 3z

Open E Minor-Shape fills

Now play these examples based around the open E Minor chord shape. With the capo on the 4th fret, this creates an G# Minor chord.

Example 3za

Example 3zb

Example 3zc

Example 3zd

Open D Minor-Shape fills

The final set of examples in this chapter are based on the open D Minor shape. Because the capo is placed at the 4th fret, it creates a F# Minor chord. Listen to the audio before playing each example.

Example 3ze

Two bars of strumming followed by two bars of single note arpeggios is a great way to mix up your rhythmic patterns.

Example 3zf

Example 3zg

Example 3zh

Essential capo listening

Here are some of my favourite guitar tracks that use a capo in on the guitar.

- John Mayer – Queen of California

- Martin Tallstrom – Summer Breeze

- The Eagles – Hotel California

- The Beatles – Here Comes the Sun

- James Taylor – Fire and Rain

- Razorlight – America

- Jeff Buckley – Hallelujah

Section Two: Blues

Chapter Four – Blues Part One

Now you have mastered the essentials of Major and Minor open chords, we will focus on combining rhythm and lead licks in a Blues context.

In this chapter, we will dissect a traditional Twelve-Bar Blues pattern in A. This pattern is the basis of thousands of Blues and Rock songs, and is the most commonly played sequence at jam sessions. By practicing all the ideas in this chapter, you will gain the confidence and fluidity to make your playing sound prepared and fluent.

For more information on the construction of a Twelve-Bar Blues check out Joseph Alexander's book. **The Complete Guide to Playing Blues Guitar Part One: Rhythm Guitar.**

Key points to focus on in this chapter

• Learn the Twelve-Bar Blues structure by heart.

• Play the Twelve-Bar Blues riffs without any lead ideas.

• Learn the lead guitar licks on their own.

• Practice alternating between a bar of riff and a bar of lead.

• Practice alternating between a bar of lead and a bar of riff.

• Play the Twelve-Bar Blues in multiple keys.

• Play with a band, or with at least one other musician.

Example 4a demonstrates a traditional Twelve-Bar Blues in the key of A. Most of the examples featured in this chapter use a shuffle rhythm. Say the phrase "chunka-chunka" to get your brain prepared for how it should be played. The most important thing to learn is how the structure of a Twelve-Bar Blues works. Spend time learning the chart below before attempting to play these examples.

Example 4a

First, let's explore a classic way to add a variation to the main riff. Although I have only written this riff in A, you can move it into D and E too, and play along with the full 12 bar blues pattern seen above.

Example 4b

This next variation is reminiscent of Eric Clapton. Make sure you move it into the keys of D and E as well, and play it through the whole Twelve-Bar Blues cycle.

Example 4c

Here is another common riff variation used by players like Stevie Ray Vaughan and B.B. King.

Example 4d

Example 4e is a fourth variation to the original Twelve-Bar Blues riff. Spend time creating your own riff patterns once you are comfortable with the patterns in this chapter.

Example 4e

Play the open A mini power-chord before adding this common blues lick in A. Listen to how I add the vibrato on the corresponding audio track.

Example 4f

Example 4g

Here is another cool idea that gets you used to alternating between a mini open A5 power-chord and a blues lick in A.

Example 4g

In a Twelve-Bar Blues progression, there is often a bar (or two) that brings the progression back to the start again this is called a 'turnaround'. Example 4h highlights the turnaround used in example 4i.

Example 4h

Now that you have mastered the rhythm and lead elements separately it is time to blend them together into a full Twelve-Bar Blues. Alternate between playing a rhythmic bar of the Twelve-Bar riff pattern, and the lead guitar fills in A, D, and E. You will notice that instead of playing all the fills in the key of A, I have moved them up the fretboard to D and E where needed in the progression.

Example 4i

E7 ... **D7** ...

```
T                    12--12----15-              10--10----13-
A             12-                        2--2--4--4-
B    2--2--4--4-                         0--0--0--0-
```

A7 ... **E7** **F7** **E7**

```
T                                                    0-
A                                               8--7- 0-
B  2--2--4--4--2--2--4--4-              8--7-
   0--0--0--0--0--0--0--0-    2-     7--6-
                             0--0-   8--7-
```

Learning patterns that use open strings is great. As set out in Chapter Three, you can use a capo to move them into different keys, however by learning a movable Twelve-Bar pattern, you can play it in any key.

To play the full Twelve-Bar Blues pattern, move the full shape to the 10th fret (6th string) for the bars of D, and the 12th fret (6th string) for bars of E. If you are unsure of the full Twelve-Bar structure, refer to the start of the chapter.

Example 4j

```
T
A
B  7--7--9--9--7--7--9--9-
   5--5--5--5--5--5--5--5-
```

Here are some licks you can use as fills in the Twelve-Bar Blues riffs. Example 4k is a classic blues-rock lick reminiscent of AC/DC that uses the A Minor Pentatonic scale.

Example 4k

Example 4l also uses the A Minor Pentatonic scale with a triplet feel. If you are struggling to count a triplet rhythm use a three-syllable word, my preference is el-e-phant.

Example 4l

Here is a lick often used by the king of Texas Blues, Stevie Ray Vaughan.

Example 4m

The final lick in this section is in the style of Eric Clapton.

Example 4n

Example 4o combines Minor Pentatonic licks, Twelve-Bar Blues riffs, and a turnaround to form a complete solo Twelve-Bar Blues piece.

Example 4o

'Riffy' Twelve-Bar Blues

In the next set of Twelve-Bar Blues patterns you will learn a riff that you can play in unison with a bass player to create a big sound.

Example 4p demonstrates a sequence using a cool riff. For those of you who play in a band, get your bass player to play this riff along with you when you practice.

Example 4p

Example 4q shows the movable Blues scale shape in the key of A.

Example 4q

We can adapt the original riff to create some interesting variations.

Example 4r

Example 4s

Here is a classic Blues scale lick used by Jimi Hendrix.

Example 4t

Example 4u and 4v demonstrate two more classic Blues-Rock licks to add to your lick arsenal.

Example 4u

Example 4v

Earlier in the chapter, I showed you how a turnaround brings the Twelve-Bar Blues progression back to bar one. Here is a turnaround using three-note '7' chords of D7, Eb7, and E7.

Example 4w

Now for the fun bit! Example 4x uses riffs, fills, and a turnaround idea to blend rhythmic and lead playing into a one-guitar arrangement.

Example 4x

Example 4y shows a double-stop fill using the A Minor Pentatonic scale on the G and B strings.

A Minor Pentatonic - G and B Strings Only

```
              3        5        7        9            12       15
```

Example 4y

TAB
```
|13----13----13----12----12----12----8-----8-----8-----7-----7-----7----|
|14----14----14----12----12----12----9-----9-----9-----7-----7-----7----|
```

My favourite way to add colour in my solos is to alternate between single-note lines and double-stops. Example 4z demonstrates this approach.

Example 4z

full

full

TAB
```
|8----8----8----7----5--------------7----5----------5------------5----|
|9----9----9----------------7--------------------------------------|
```

In bar one of example 4za, I created a double-stop lick around the A Blues scale. In bar two I created a turnaround that used an E7#9 chord. This is commonly referred to as the 'Hendrix chord'.

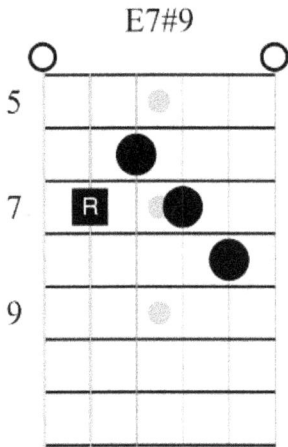

Example 4za

Example 4zb combines all the ideas from the second half of this chapter to form a Twelve-Bar Blues arrangement. I recommend listening to the audio track a few times before leaving this example.

Example 4zb

By now, you should feel comfortable with the Twelve-Bar Blues structure, how to create riffs, and blend them with licks. The Twelve-Bar Blues will form the basis for many future chapters, so make sure it feels comfortable before you move on.

Chapter Five – Minor Blues

A popular modification of the traditional Twelve-Bar Blues is a Minor Blues. The darker, sadder tone this produces has been popular with guitarists who prefer to solo using Minor scales. Before moving through the examples in this chapter, check out the blues classic The Thrill Is Gone by Blues guitar legend B.B. King, to give you an idea of how a minor Blues chord sounds.

Goals for this chapter

• Listen to the examples at least twice before playing them.

• Learn the Minor Blues structure by heart.

• Play the Minor Blues arpeggios on their own.

• Learn the lead guitar licks on their own.

• Practice alternating between a bar of arpeggio and a bar of lead.

• Practice alternating between a bar of lead and a bar of arpeggio.

• Play half a bar of arpeggio and half a bar of lead.

• Play half a bar of lead and half a bar of arpeggio.

• Play the Minor Blues in multiple keys.

• Play with a band, or at least one other musician.

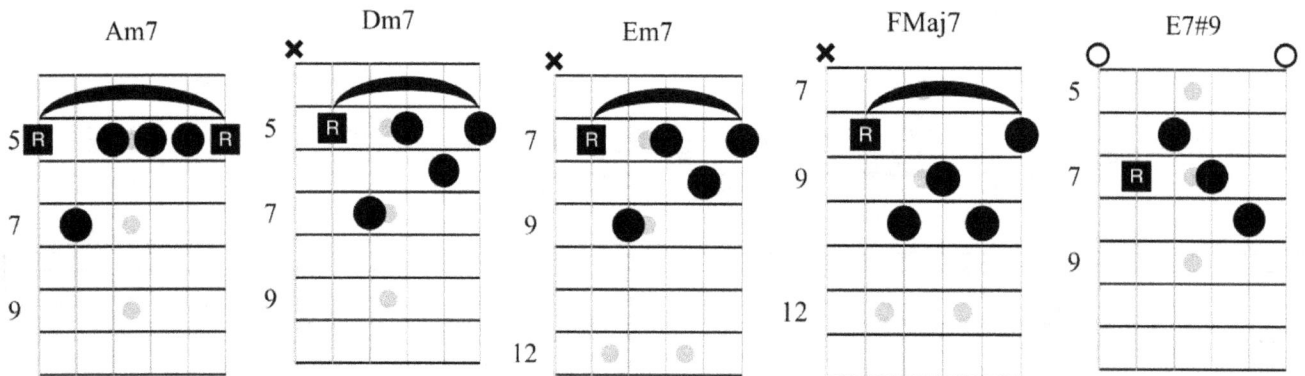

Example 5a shows the Twelve-Bar Minor Blues chords in the key of A. It uses the chords of A Minor 7, D Minor 7, E Minor 7, F Major 7, and E7#9. If you are unfamiliar with these barre chord shapes, look at the neck diagrams above and learn the shapes before continuing.

Example 5a

One way to liven up your rhythm guitar chops is to use arpeggio patterns. An arpeggio is simply a broken chord, so anytime you pick the notes of a chord individually you are playing an arpeggio. As always, start off slowly with a metronome and build accuracy before speeding up.

Example 5b

The minor pentatonic and Blues scales can both be used to accompany the Minor Blues progression. For variation, I have included the A Natural Minor scale (A B C D E F G) which has a darker tone than its Pentatonic counterpart. Check out the classic solo from Stairway to Heaven by Led Zeppelin for many tasty A Natural Minor licks.

A Natural Minor

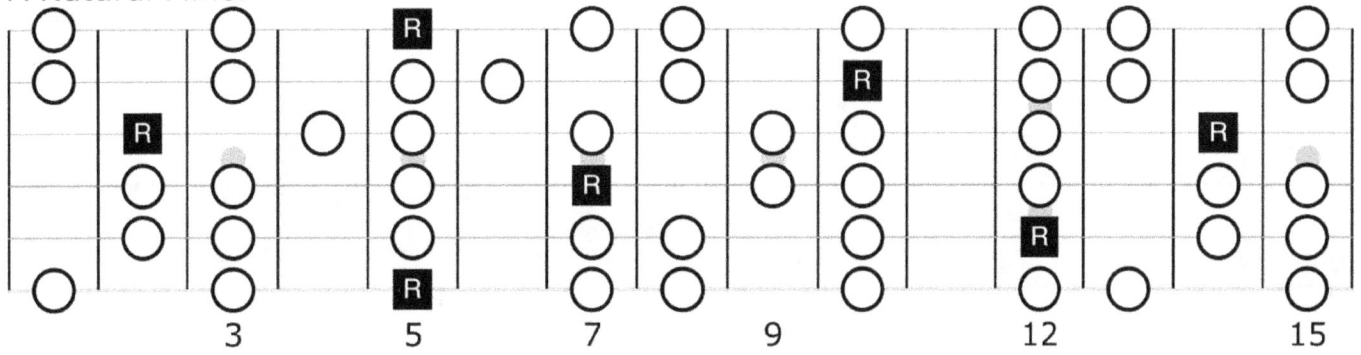

Example 5c

This lick combines the A Natural Minor scale and the A Blues scale to form a slippery Blues-Rock lick.

Example 5d

By taking the same pattern of notes through multiple octaves you can create longer lines in your soloing. Example 5e uses the A Blues scale to achieve this.

Example 5e

Example 5f uses the notes C, E, and G to create an A Minor 7th arpeggio before using the A Blues scale to complete and end the lick.

Example 5f

Play this A Minor Pentatonic double-stop lick on the B and E strings. Be sure not to overshoot the slide between the 8th and 10th frets.

Example 5g

Here is a bluesy double-stop lick that uses the A Natural Minor scale (A B C D E F G) on the G and B strings.

Example 5h

In example 5i, I created a double-stop phrase based around an E Minor 7 chord in the style of Jimi Hendrix.

Example 5i

By adding a slide, arpeggio and string-skip to an E7#9 chord you can create an interesting lick with little effort.

Example 5j

In example 5k I have introduced what I call the 'Django Reinhardt technique'. By playing a semi-tone (one fret) below each of the notes of the E7#9 before resolving to a chord tone you can create a jazzy sound. You can play a semi-tone above each note of the chord too.

Example 5k

Now that you have learnt some chords and licks in a Minor Blues progression, it is time to put it all together. Be sure to start off slowly, at around 50 beats-per-minute with a metronome. Only raise the tempo of the metronome when you can play everything perfectly.

Example 5l is my favourite example in this book and is something I play regularly as a warm up.

Example 5l

So far, I have concentrated on building the fundamentals of good rhythm and lead fills in one key. As you develop in blending rhythm and lead guitar, you will find that you can often use different scales within one piece of music. Our Minor Blues progression is in the key of A Minor, however it contains two other Minor chords: D Minor and E Minor. Instead of playing A Minor fills over those bars, you can play D Minor fills over the D Minor, and E Minor fills over the E Minor chords.

Shown below in example 5n is the D Blues scale (D F G Ab A C) with a root note on the A string.

Example 5m

Play the E Blues scale (E G A Bb B D) from the 7th fret of the A String. Notice it is the same scale as the previous example played two frets higher.

Example 5n

Here is a D Minor lick.

Example 5o

This bluesy D Minor lick is reminiscent of Mark Knopfler's playing.

Example 5p

One of my favourite things about the guitar is that when you learn one new lick, you can play it in any key just by starting at a different fret. Here is that D Minor lick played in E Minor.

Example 5q

My students like to 'steal my licks', and this is a classic A Blues scale lick I use all the time.

Example 5r

Here is another A Blues lick, this time in the style of John Mayer.

Example 5s

Earlier, I showed how to solo over an E7#9 chord by approaching each of the chord tones from a semi-tone below or above. A common trick is to combine these approaches.

Example 5t

Half a bar of lead lines mixed with half a bar of arpeggios is another way to create melodic excitement. Look at how I do this in example 5v.

Example 5u

Dm7
¼
full
Dm7
full
Am7
full
full
½
Am7
Fmaj7
full
Em7
Fmaj7
E7#9
TAB

Chapter Six – Gospel Blues

It's now time to play another popular blues structure: Gospel Blues. Once again, I have written this in the key of A, but you can move this pattern into any key you wish.

Before you rush into learning the fills and licks, spend time mastering the chord shapes shown below. Remember that the rhythmic element is the most important part, with the fills acting as the icing on the cake.

Make it a priority to listen to the accompanying audio tracks before you learn each example. This will help you rely on your ear more heavily. Remember: if it sounds good, it is good.

Essential elements from this chapter

• Learn the Gospel Blues chords.

• Learn the Gospel Blues progression.

• Become familiar with rhythmic variations of the Gospel Blues progression.

• Learn the A Mixolydian, D Mixolydian, and E Mixolydian scale shapes.

• Play the licks written in A Mixolydian, D Mixolydian, and E Mixolydian scale shapes.

• Create your own licks in the Mixolydian scale shapes.

• Have fun combining the Gospel Blues chords with new lick vocabulary.

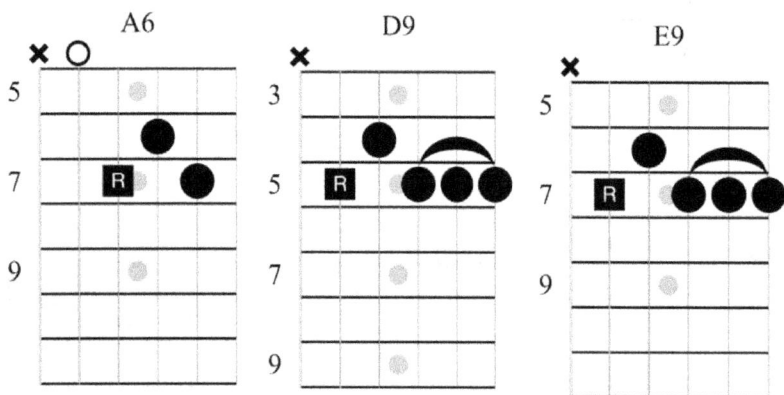

Example 6a shows the full Twelve-Bar Gospel Blues chord sequence played with one chord per bar.

Example 6a

You can play the root note on its own before sliding and arpeggiating each chord. Example 6b brings life to the Gospel Blues progression.

Example 6b

The A Mixolydian scale (A B C# D E F# G) is a perfect complement to the Gospel Blues chord progression.

Example 6c

A Mixolydian Lick Vocabulary

Listen to the audio, then learn these four Mixolydian licks that can be used with the Gospel Blues chord progression.

Example 6d

Example 6e

Example 6f

Example 6g

Now you have learnt these A Mixolydian licks, it is time to blend them into the chords of the Gospel Blues. Start slowly at around 50 beats per minute as there is a lot of information here.

Example 6h

Over the D9 chords you can use the D Mixolydian scale.

Example 6i

D Mixolydian Scale Licks

Add these D Mixolydian licks into your vocabulary.

Example 6j

Example 6k

Over the bars of E9 in the Gospel Blues progression you can play the E Mixolydian scale.

Example 6l

E Mixolydian Scale Licks

Learn these two E Mixolydian scale licks that can be played over any E9 bar.

Example 6m

Example 6n

Example 6o combines everything in this chapter. I start with a lead lick and alternate between half a bar of lead and half a bar of rhythm. You can, of course, play this the other way around, or alternate between full bars of rhythm and lead.

Example 6o

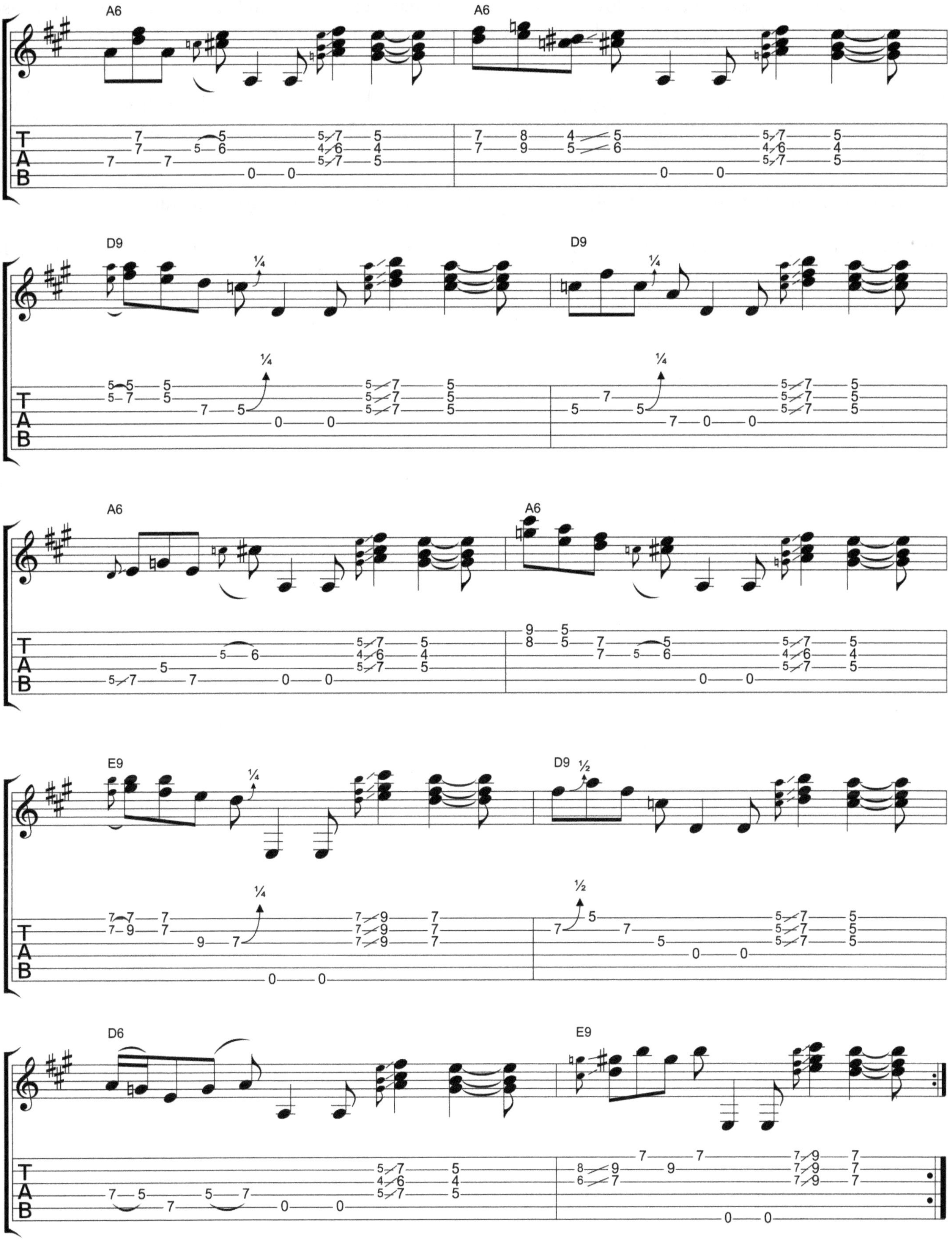
A6
A6
D9
D9
A6
A6
E9
D9
D6
E9

Begin by playing each example very slowly with the metronome set at 50bpm, and make sure that each note is clean and clear. Watch your picking hand and notice if you are applying the strict 'down, up' alternate picking required.

When you can play an example perfectly three times in a row at 50bpm, try raising the metronome speed to 53bpm. Continue to increase the metronome speed in increments of 3 beats per minute up to a target speed of 80bpm+.

This form of practice means that you only increase the speed once the lick is played accurately.

I use the Tempo app (made by Frozen Ape) on my phone. I know I will always have my phone with me, so I never have an excuse to practice without a metronome.

Section 3: Rock
Chapter Seven – Two-Note Power Chords

The third section in this book focuses on blending rhythm and lead in rock guitar. In this chapter, I will show you how to build awesome rock progressions that use two-note power chords. When written in a chord, a '5' dictates that it is a power chord. Power chords can be used to replace both Major and Minor chords. For example, a D5 power chord could replace either a D Major or D Minor chord.

In the following examples you will use a D Minor Pentatonic scale between the chords to create mini fills and licks.

Like all chords on the guitar, there are multiple ways that power chords can be played. Shown in example 7a is the D5 power chord shape with a root on the E, A, and D strings. Let's dive in!

Example 7a

Played between the power chords of D5, C5, Bb5 and C5 are four muted strums to give the progression a percussive feel. Sometimes a percussive fill creates just as much excitement as one based around a lick.

Example 7b

Example 7c demonstrates the chord progression with all the power chords played on the 5th string.

Example 7c

Now play the progression with the power chords on the D string.

Example 7d

Example 7e demonstrates the D Minor Pentatonic scale, which will be used for the fills in the rest of this chapter.

Example 7e

By adding a note between each of the chords we can create a 'call and response' pattern. The power chords call out and the note of F responds.

Example 7f

In beat four of example 7g we add a hammer-on fill.

Example 7g

This example alternates between a pull-off and a hammer-on pattern.

Example 7h

Slides are an excellent tool to add melodic interest between chords:

Example 7i

Example 7j shows another slide example with the fills on the G and B strings.

Example 7j

Bends are a rock staple! Adding them into this sequence sounds awesome. If you want more information on all types of bends be sure to check out my book Melodic Rock Soloing for Guitar.

Example 7k

I recommend practicing the bends in example 7l on their own before including them with the subsequent examples.

Example 7l

The following two examples use double-stops between each power chord.

Example 7m

Example 7n

Next, the fills come before the power chords. Example 7o shows this with by adding vibrato on the note F.

Example 7o

In example 7p, play the legato fills before the power chords.

Example 7p

If you are struggling to make the transitions clean between fills and chords, slow down and practice them individually before linking them together.

Example 7q

Using bends before power chords can sound raw and aggressive.

Example 7r

I absolutely love sliding double-stops, and they are one of my favourite ways to create fills between chords. Example 7s demonstrates this idea before each power chord.

Example 7s

As well as playing the D Minor Pentatonic scale with the root note on the E string, it is important to learn it with a root note on the A string.

Example 7t

Next, I pick my favourite patterns and play them with an A string root to show you how to play in different areas of the fretboard.

Example 7u

Example 7v

Example 7w

Example 7x

Popular Power Chord Songs

• White Stripes – Seven Nation Army (If played in standard tuning)

• Green Day – American Idiot

• The Kinks – You Really Got Me

• Blink-182 – All the Small Things

• Lenny Kravitz – Fly Away

• Nirvana – Smells like Teen Spirit

• Scorpions – Rock You Like a Hurricane

Check them out and apply the techniques shown in this chapter.

Chapter Eight – Power Chords Part Two

In this chapter, I will show you how to create three-note power chords and alternate between rhythm patterns and lead fills.

The three-note power chord sounds fuller than its two-note counterpart, and lends itself more to overdriven or distorted tones. Being a proficient power chord player is one of the most useful abilities to have at a jam session.

The examples in this chapter are in the key of B, and show both Minor and Major examples of how to use power chords and fills.

Example 8a shows how to play a B5 power chord with the root note on the E, A, D, and G-strings. The shapes played on the D and the G-strings may feel less familiar to you but are equally useful.

Example 8a

The next examples show three different ways to play the same power chord sequence of B5, G5, D5, and A5. Playing power chord sequences in a variety of ways can help break any ruts you may be caught in.

Example 8b

Example 8c

Example 8d

Example 8e demonstrates all four shapes of the B5, G5, D5, and A5 power chords. From this you can create your own patterns and link them up how you wish.

Example 8e

B Minor Lick Vocabulary

In the next few examples you will build up some core rock licks to blend with rock power chords. As well as using the ideas I have shown, try to make up your own.

Example 8f demonstrates a classic blues-rock lick used by guitarists such as Angus Young and Joe Satriani. Use the neck diagram of the B Minor Pentatonic scale as reference.

B Minor Pentatonic

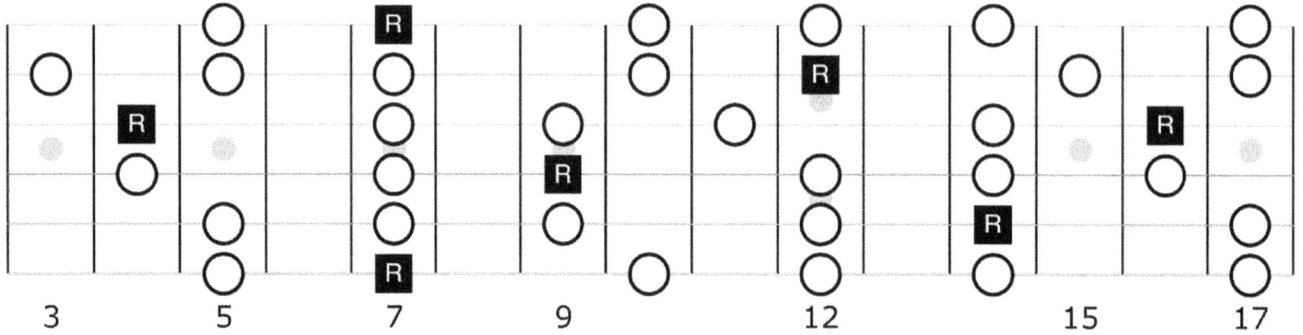

Example 8f

Here is another classic bluesy lick that is synonymous with B.B. King.

Example 8g

The B Natural Minor scale adds the notes C# and G to the B Minor Pentatonic scale and has a classic rock sound. The next two examples use this scale.

B Natural Minor

Example 8h

Example 8i

Example 8j

Example 8k

Example 8l

Example 8m

By using a string-skip between the D and the B strings, this lick adds melodic interest to the B Blues scale.

Example 8n

For more licks in this style be sure to check out my book **Melodic Rock Soloing for Guitar**.

Example 8o

If you have worked methodically throughout the book, you will now be aware that playing one bar of rhythm followed by a bar of lead works well. Bars one and three show a B5 and D5 power chord played with a classic rock rhythm. Bars two and four use licks around the B Minor Pentatonic and Blues scales.

Example 8p

As guitarists we tend to spend time focussing on Minor sounds, but it is important to know how to play Major progressions too. Example 8q shows a chord progression of B5, F#5, G#5, and E5, a common pop-rock pattern. Remember, what I have written is only a guide, you can change any example to fit your own taste.

Example 8q

B Major Lick Vocabulary

Learn the following licks based around the B Major scale with the neck diagram below as a reference.

B Major Pentatonic

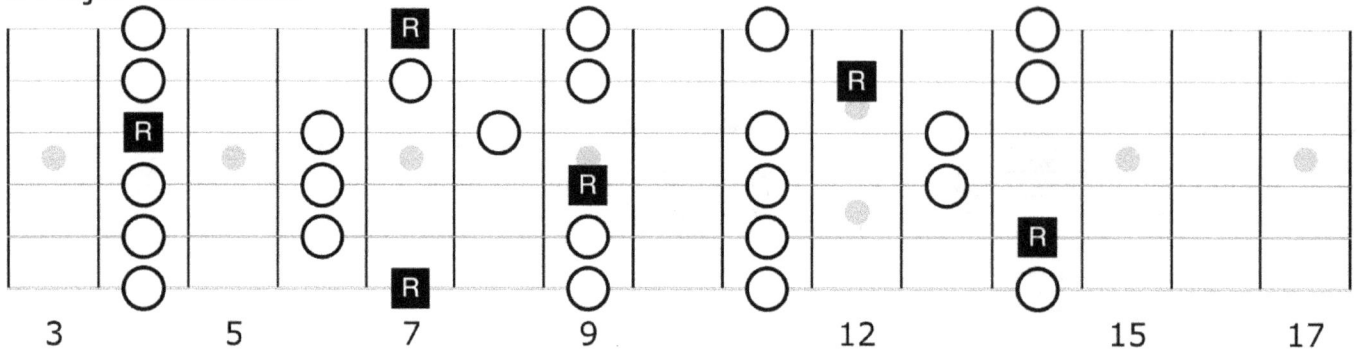

Example 8r

Example 8s

Begin slowly and follow the picking instructions when playing the legato patterns in the next two examples. Use a metronome at around 50bpm and only speed it up when you can play the example perfectly three times in a row.

Example 8t

Example 8u

This simple double-stop lick is easy to remember and will work brilliantly as a fill between power chords.

Example 8v

Example 8w

Example 8x

Example 8y

Example 8z combines the Major power chord sequence of B5, F#5, G#5, E5, with a mixture of B Major Pentatonic licks and phrases from earlier in the chapter.

Example 8z

An extremely cool variation to the standard power chord shape is what I refer to as 'The add9 power chord'. Andy Summers made this shape famous in Message in a Bottle by The Police. The add9 power chord sounds great with or without distortion, and can also be used to replace Major or Minor chords. Simply put, you add the 9th note of the Major Scale to the original chord. In the case of B, it is the note of C#.

For more information on music theory check out Joseph Alexander's book **Modern Music Theory for Guitarists.**

Example 8za

Another power chord you can experiment with is demonstrated in example 8zb. Popular with rock and pop bands, this three-note power chord shape has a fat sound to it. You can think of it as a two-note E5 power chord with B as the bass note.

Example 8zb

Example 8zc demonstrates a chord sequence in the style of The Police using an arpeggio pattern. I recommend playing the middle note of the chords with your second finger, rather than your third.

Example 8zc

When I was studying at the Guitar Institute, I wrote this riff called Space Travel. It combines Badd9 and Gadd9 power chords with fills in B Minor. Pay close attention to the picking directions I have included.

Example 8zd

I call the following two-note power-chord shape the 'Brian May passing chord', as I first came across it in the tune One Vision by Queen. Instead of getting caught up in the name, think of it as a passing chord in B Minor. This will become clearer when used in context.

Example 8ze

This example to combines a two-note B5 power chord, the Brian May passing chord, and a fill in the B Minor Pentatonic scale.

Example 8zf

Here is the same riff shifted up a string.

Example 8zg

Now, play the same sequence but with root notes on the D string.

Example 8zh

To show how many ways one power chord sequence can be played on the guitar, play the power chord riff with the root notes on the G string.

Example 8zi

Here is the Brian May passing chord as a three-note shape.

Example 8zj

Power chords, percussive muted strums, and a B Minor Pentatonic fill make up this rocky four-bar phrase.

Example 8zk

A good way to punctuate a power chord sequence is to add a fill at the end of each bar. Even just one note played with vibrato can add excitement to your playing.

Example 8zl

The final example in this chapter uses a B Major power chord sequence with fills from the B Major Pentatonic scale.

Example 8zm

There is an enormous amount of information in this chapter, so keep returning to it over time. Find some songs that use power chords and start to add fills and patterns between them. This will make a huge difference to your practice regimes, your jam sessions, and your own riff writing process.

Chapter Nine – Drone Notes

A 'drone' is a note that rings continually underneath other notes. The idea in this chapter is to play an open string note and let it ring for as long as possible. The drone acts as a root note for you to base your lead licks around.

The majority of examples in this chapter are played over a droning open low E string combined with the E Blues, E Major, and E Mixolydian scales. Once you become familiar with these scales and how to drone notes, feel free to expand them to any other scale patterns and shapes you enjoy playing.

In example 9a I have written a multi-octave E Blues scale with a ringing low E string. Let it ring under as much of the scale as possible. You may need to re-pick the low E to keep it sounding as you go through the scale. Listen to the audio track to see how I achieve this.

Example 9a

Bands like Metallica often use drone notes under power chords to create a powerful effect. Example 9b demonstrates this with an E Blues scale fill.

Example 9b

The E7#9 chord is synonymous with Jimi Hendrix and is often simply called 'the Hendrix chord'. This Hendrix-style vamp blends drone notes, the Hendrix chord, E Blues scale fills, and two-note power chords.

Example 9c

Example 9d demonstrates the triads (chords with only three notes) of E Minor, D, and C, and fills the gaps with the E Blues scale. Study the diagrams below to see how I turned full barre chord shapes into the triads you see in the example.

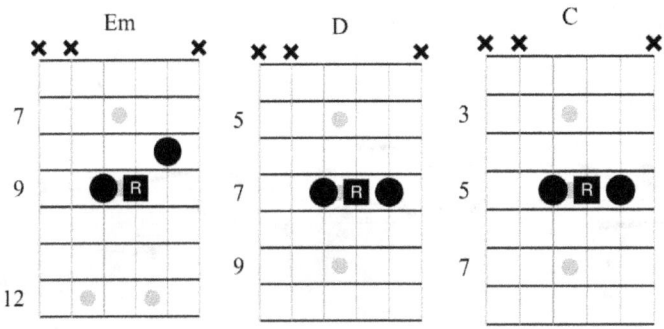

Example 9d

In the next example, I show you how to apply double-stop patterns using the E Blues scale over the low E string drone note.

Example 9e

Now examine a multi-octave E Major scale and let the open E string ring as long as possible. Re-pick the string if the note dies out.

Example 9f

This E Major scale lick combines slides and legato over the ringing low E drone note.

Example 9g

An open low E string drone is played in the song Buck Rogers by Feeder. This example is in the style of the opening riff to that track and includes slides and vibrato.

Example 9h

The next example sounds good when played with either fingerpicking or hybrid picking (pick and fingers). The combination of the ringing drone note, double-stops, and 12th fret harmonics creates a flowing pop-rock idea.

Example 9i

In music, there are three main types of chords; Minor, Major, and Dominant. The E Blues scale will work perfectly over all E Minor Chords, the E Major scale will work over all E Major chords and the E Mixolydian scale will work on E Dominant chords.

By playing scales with a drone note and learning multi-octave scale shapes, you can break out of any box-shaped ruts you have been stuck in.

Example 9j demonstrates a multi-octave E Mixolydian scale with a low E as a drone note.

Example 9j

Example 9k is reminiscent of Slash's playing. It has a funk-rock feel and uses drone notes with the E Mixolydian scale.

Example 9k

When first learning example 9l, ignore the muted X notes. Listen to the rhythm played on the audio and play through the example without the mutes. As you become comfortable with that pattern, add the muted strums back in.

Example 9l

Years ago, when Dubstep became popular, I was challenged by a music producer to write a guitar part that would fit alongside the various loud growling tones he was creating. I used a droning open D, and a sliding pattern that outlined the chords of D Minor, Bb, and C.

I called this piece Dub City. Let the open D string ring out as much as possible and make the slides clean and precise. Use the examples featured in this chapter to create your own piece that revolves around an open string drone. Remember, if you can't find an open string note to fit the key you need, you can use a capo.

Example 9m

Congratulations! You made it! I hope you have discovered a wealth of new ideas for blending rhythm and lead guitar that you can keep coming back to for years. Like everything with guitar playing, these techniques do require work but as I always say, "The more time you devote to playing your guitar, the better friend it will be".

Checklist

Now that you have completed the book, test yourself to see if you can do the following things without referring to the corresponding chapter. If not, no need to worry; just go back and refresh your knowledge of that technique.

• Can you blend licks with open Major and Minor chords?

• Can you use a capo and create ringing chord sequences using it anywhere on the guitar?

• Do you understand the Twelve-Bar Blues structure?

• Can you play standard, Minor and Gospel Blues progressions?

• Are you confident with two-note and three-note power chords, their construction and how to apply them?

Monitoring your progress on the guitar is very important and often overlooked. Keep coming back to this checklist and work on the areas you feel are weak, instead of always concentrating on the stronger aspects of your playing.

Conclusion

By now, you are probably swimming in a sea of new ideas and possibilities. I recommend you create your own personal video lick diary for reference. Film your licks and, if possible, write them out in standard notation or tab. That way, when you look back in six months' time, not only can you see and hear how far your playing has come, you can revisit licks that you may have forgotten.

Practice what you don't know, not what you do! This is quite simply the best advice I can give any musician. Use a metronome to help you master each example and use backing tracks to create a more musical approach to practicing.

An important goal is to play with other people, so while you are developing your skills find time to jam with other people. Playing with other musicians is the best way to improve your playing.

Be sure to check out my other titles also published by Fundamental Changes:

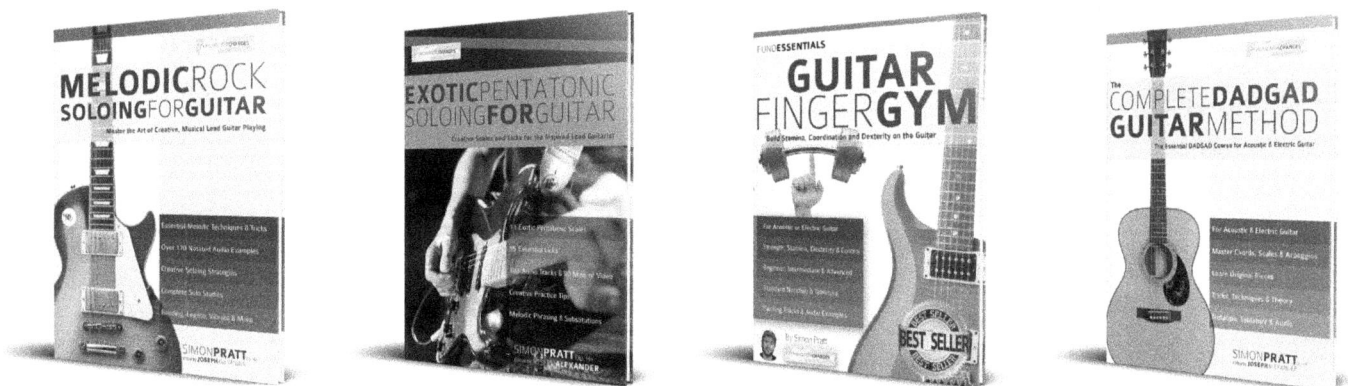

You can get them all here: **www.fundamental-changes.com/book**

My passion in life is teaching people to play and express themselves through the guitar. If you have any questions, please get in touch and I will do my best to respond as quickly as possible.

You can contact me on **simeypratt@gmail.com** or via the **Fundamental Changes YouTube channel**.

Have fun!

Pop Quiz Answers

• E G A Bb B D

• Two notes played at the same time

• Start off at around 50 beats-per-minute with a metronome before speeding up

• A C D Eb E G

www.ingramcontent.com/pod-product-compliance
Lightning Source LLC
Chambersburg PA
CBHW081427090426
42740CB00017B/3213